WORDS for the UNKNOWN

AS YOU GO

TANNER OLSON

As You Go: Words for the Unknown By Tanner Olson
Writtentospeak.com

© 2020 by Tanner Olson

All rights reserved. No part of this publication
may be reproduced, stored in a retrieval system,
or transmitted in any form or by any means
- electronic, mechanical, digital, photocopy,
recording, or any other - except for quotations in
printed reviews, without the prior permission of the
author or publisher.

Cover Illustration and Design: James Saleska
Jamessaleska.com

ISBN: 978-0-578-69795-6

This book goes great with coffee.

i wrote this for you

I'm just happy to be here.

INTRODUCTION

At the time I was first writing this, I was months from turning thirty years-old. And at the time of editing this, I am 30 years old.
Life comes at you fast.
If I were to tell 12-year-old Tanner I am 30, he would call me old.

12-year-old Tanner was rude.

But, I don't feel old.

I feel tired, but not old.
I feel stretched, but not old.
I feel like I've survived something, but not old.
I feel many things, which is why I write poetry, but old is not one of the things I feel.
Except my knees.
My knees feel like they are 87. So if you purchased this book, know that your money is going to my knee replacements.

And maybe a dog.
Hopefully a dog.

As I was making my way through my 20s, stumbling and running, taking steps forward, backward, and to the left, I began to realize that none of us know what we are doing.

We are all doing something, but do any of us really, truly know what we are doing?

AS YOU GO

I don't think so.

Even the people who *seem* to have it all together don't. They are just like you and me, making it up as they go, but perhaps with more confidence or a bigger bank account.

This might sound hopeless or bleak, but truthfully, this thought, that none of us really know what we are doing, gave me comfort as I made my way through my twenties and into my thirties.

There is freedom found in knowing I'm not the only one who feels lost or unsure.

There is a calming peace that comes when someone older than me reminds me they don't know what's going on either.

Although none of us really know what we are doing, this doesn't mean we should stop *doing*.
We are still here.
We are still trying.
We are still moving forward or backward or wherever.

As I've made my way through these past few years, I've been writing a few words down:
poems, prayers, and wonderings.
Little reminders to remember; short thoughts to hold onto as I go into the daily unknown.
This book is not a map or textbook, but perhaps it can serve as a place to rest as you go.

These words can sit with you when you feel hopeless or lost or alone or turned around.

These words can silence the noise with peace.

These words can bring light to the darkness.

Take your time as you make your way through this book.

There is no need to rush to the next page.

AS YOU GO

See, no need to rush.

Read slow.

Give it time.

Let the words meet you where you are.

Pray them. Sit with them. Share them.

If one of these pages fills you with joy, take out your phone and share some hope with the world.

Pick up these words when you need to, and put them down when it's time to get up and continue.

There are no rules for this book.

Start in the very middle if you'd like.

This is now your book.

These words are for you.

And I hope that is freeing for you.

AS YOU GO

We may not have everything figured out, but we can make time to breathe, reflect, and restart.

It is my hope and prayer that this little book will bring you comfort as you go.

And as you go, remember you aren't going alone.

We are going together.

TANNER OLSON

AS YOU GO
WORDS *for the* UNKNOWN

by
TANNER OLSON

as you go
may it be faith
that leads you
through the
unknown

as you go
may it be hope
that keeps you
moving through every
yes and every no

as you go
may it be love
you leave behind
so others may know
so others may grow
so others may go

AS YOU GO

i just need to
breathe
and be
breathe
and be
breathe
and be
i just need to

step into it.
the unknown.
the uncertain.
the wilderness.
the dream.
and you'll see
fear was never
a good enough reason
to keep you
from living free.

AS YOU GO

i want to leave behind
something
that will get
you ahead
planting seeds of hope
with my life
so our children can climb to the peak
of what we planted beneath

You're all i've ever known
and for all i don't know
i'll hold fast to
a faithfulness
that goes beyond
an aching past

AS YOU GO

in a season of silence
i'm searching for something
spoken to grasp
to be met with a reminder
that this too will pass

i've been trying to pray
but most days
i've got nothing to say
so i smile
with my eyes
and keep them to the sky
watching and waiting
and
it's not that i don't want to talk
to God
but i'm learning to believe praying
doesn't always mean talking
and i'm beginning
to sit still and
listen
to listen still with
a smile on my face
below the sky
watching and waiting
because one day
i'll have something to say

create growth
with love
like you're
five again
and she
asks, "are
you okay?"

eyes open
accepting

palms face up
inviting

mouth closed
listening

hold steady
loving

AS YOU GO

it's not what i thought
it'd be
it's different
but
it's good
it's good
but
it's different
it's a different kind of good

maybe i need
a moment
or two
to sit and be
to sit and be
with You

AS YOU GO

the old me
got me
to this me
and i wouldn't be
this me
if it wasn't for
you

place that spark back in my eye
the one that would light up
when i'd ask why
the one that went out
when i waved goodbye
to the child
and wonder
and dreams
that once lived inside

AS YOU GO

maybe today is the new beginning
you've been praying for
maybe today is the new beginning
you've been hoping for
maybe today is the new beginning
you've been preparing for
maybe today is the new beginning
you've been reaching for
maybe today is the day.
and i think it might just be.

learning to breathe
and let it be
to continue walking
light and free
like this is what
You've always had for me

because

this is what
You've always
had for me

AS YOU GO

fingertips on keys
because
it's hard for me to speak
i write to keep
from living beneath
everything
inside of
me

keep me brave
as i seek to find
what's hidden behind
your wild eyes

AS YOU GO

or
or i can say
i am thankful
words to remind
this is not the end
and there is good
and i am
simply on the mend

frustration and thankfulness
battle for space
i'm caught in the middle
willing to fight
for the word on the right

AS YOU GO

where there is peace
is where i want to be found
and when i return
i'll bring peace
as if i'm bound
to this growing ground

i'll hold on with
both hands
even when i don't
understand
but i know You're good
and through it all
i am somehow
understood

AS YOU GO

i'm asking

where
are
You

with eyes closed
because
i don't need to see

i already know

You heard me when
and You hear me now
and i know there are
no empty words
that fall from
this mouth

AS YOU GO

stand with the hurting
stand with the broken
stand with the outcast
stand with each other
we remain
together for each other

let it be
let me go
let me be
not afraid
to be
me
as i go

AS YOU GO

deep is my trust
for the hope
beyond
all of this

i need the
silence and
stillness to
remember and
restore to
get up
and
go

AS YOU GO

falling and rising
and i'm somewhere
in between
but i guess this is
just called
living
and i'm going to keep
doing the thing

it's all heavy
and fragile
but i don't fear
the break
like i don't
scare during
the wait

AS YOU GO

a little more kindness
a lot less hate
a little more together
a lot less alone

hold me still
so i can catch
the silence
and
the humble words
that fall in the quiet

AS YOU GO

i've yet to find
the final piece
of the puzzle
but the
photo
feels whole
and today
so do i

what do You have for me
i'm just wondering
i am
but am i
going the right direction
or am i just going
what do You have for me
i'm just wondering

i'm always just wondering.

AS YOU GO

i've got to be honest
i don't know
what this poem means
or if it's a poem
but i'm not done
writing
like
i'm not done
living

it starts with
surrendering
the laying down
the letting go
the constant echo
of i don't know
the face down
eyes up
hold still
listen
and then
then i'll
go

AS YOU GO

i'm feeding fear
spoonfuls of
silence
stuffing the dark
with the light
calming the chaos
with pieces of
promises

we can't have it all
but we've been given
today
and today is
enough to
wake the wonder
within and
today is
a good enough reason
to begin again

The most powerful prayer
I've ever been encouraged
to pray was not long or poetic.
It was short.
But full.
It was quiet.
But quite loud.
Simple.
But deep.
It was one word.

Father.

Father.

One word.

A prayer of hope.
A prayer of desperation.
A prayer of surrender.
A prayer reaching with an extended and open and honest hand.
A prayer overshadowing doubt with grace.
A prayer shining like a light in the fog.
A prayer bringing peace to the silence.
A prayer of power and honesty.
A prayer that says it all.

Father.

AS YOU GO

You make something
out of nothing
as if it is nothing
but beauty
is certainly
something
and
certainly
we are not
nothing

from
everything
to
nothing

and even the
honest pause

in-between

beginning
to
end
but God
to
amen
i'm beginning to believe
You want to hear
from me

AS YOU GO

wearing fear
when all i've wanted
is to clothe myself in
stain free
peace
head to toe
with what You've
spoken over me

i'm up
again
hoping again
i could
begin again
but again
i'm up
again
reminding myself
again and again
this is not
the end

AS YOU GO

hold tight to
the echo
of forever
like it was never meant
to be
let go
because
it was never meant
to be
let go.

despite the storm
she stepped into
the wild
unknown
uncertain
but certain
she would
grow

AS YOU GO

i don't feel You

are You still
with me

i don't see You

are You still
next to me

i don't hear You

are You still
speaking to me

okay.
good.

i want to live
in the middle
of a hallelujah chorus
with voices and eyes
angled toward
forever
whispering loud for
heaven to come
down

AS YOU GO

not every thought
in my head
i believe
sometimes
i ask them
how did you
who let you
when did you
get inside
and then
i ask them to
go.

go.

waking overwhelmed
to go above and beyond
but i'm breaking beneath
whispering for peace
i'm just trying to be me
but everyday i strive to be
everyone and everything
all of this striving
is leaving me starving
so one more time
just one more time
(today)
will You remind me
i am
forgiven
and
free?

AS YOU GO

she asked
what do i do
with the love
i have

and i still
don't know
what to say

when i thought i
reached the end,
i heard You say,
"let's begin"
and that's when
You took my hand

AS YOU GO

use it for good
and let it go
pass it on for another to find
it is with this life
that i'll leave
love behind

i know
i won't grow
if i don't open up
these hands
and let go

AS YOU GO

i want to love
even when
it's loud
and
hold onto hope
when it cannot be
found

when life feels like
the wilderness
i'll look to my hands
and
trace the lines as
i pray those
ten lines
to remember
Your Kingdom
come
Your will be
done.
and i
i am far from
done.

i am far from
done.

AS YOU GO

lift up my eyes
from this floor
give me peace
as i explore
knowing where
i go
You've been
before

i'm tired
of trying to be
everyone and anything
to everyone and everything
will You remind me
You created me to
only be
only me
i can only be me.

AS YOU GO

i guess i am a little scared to ask why
a little fearful to try
a little hesitant to open my eyes
but still You stand by my side

Your faithfulness
isn't a season
it is a constant
and i am constantly
amazed by
Your faithfulness

AS YOU GO

maybe this is
what it means
to believe
and be
and maybe
this is what
it feels like for these
feet to
have faith
and for these
hands to
hold hope
and maybe this is
what i need
to move forward

disturb the darkness with the light
break the night
with a love that stretches
from left to right

AS YOU GO

together
we have come a long way
together
we have a reason to stay
together

You've taken me this far
and there is still
some road ahead
and there is still
hope to spread
and there is still
love to give
and i know
You'll be with me
until the very end.

AS YOU GO

and when i say
let it be

i'll do just that

i'll let it be
and i'll hand all of this over
to all of You
and let it be.

i will let it be.

clarity isn't required
faith is
answers aren't needed
hope is
certainty isn't given
love is

AS YOU GO

a little love
a little hope
a little is enough
to go a little further

it's Your softness
that moved me beyond my past
and that's when i asked
is this what it feels like to be free?

AS YOU GO

teach me to sing Your song slower
so i can sit longer with Your words
so i can lose myself in Your melody
so i can be found in Your faithfulness

i'm going with the grace
that got me here
the grace that led me through
kept me through
and will see me through
what i am going through

AS YOU GO

i'll keep close
the peace
You promise
and leave far behind the fear
You called us from

or
or i could breathe
and remember
You are in control
of every little thing

AS YOU GO

slowly i'm beginning
to believe and see
beauty
is what You have for me

TANNER OLSON

i've searched far and wide
and through it all
the answer has been
by my side

AS YOU GO

this is for now
but not forever
and this
like grace
is what i need to
remember

some days
it's hard to be here
but love is here
hope is here
You are here
today is here
and i guess here
is where i should be.

i should be here.

AS YOU GO

whatever this is
and whatever may be
may it only and always
be for the One
who has set me free.

i don't have all the answers
but i have love
and that's what i'll give

AS YOU GO

all of me
for all of You
all of me
from all of You
all of me
before all of You

You are who
You say You are
and
i am
in the palm
of Your hand
and
when i don't get it
You still somehow
understand
and i am still
somehow
in Your hand

AS YOU GO

whatever this is
and whatever may be
may it only and always
be for Thee

quiet my mind to
see with both eyes
that peace is found
in Who found me
and He found me

AS YOU GO

and it is in hope that i will grow.
and it is in hope that i will stay.
and it is in hope that i will remain.

but i know
the seasons will change
and the sky will rain
the fog will clear
and love
will cast out fear
and
i know
somehow
someway
i'll be okay

AS YOU GO

for all i have done
for all i have felt
for all i have feared
there is grace
there is hope
there is love
there is more to the story

and i've stepped past the start
and i'm just trying
to chase after God's own heart
and i'm just trying to not
fall apart

AS YOU GO

i'm finding beauty
in where i've been
i'm looking back
to move forward again
i'm beginning to
believe i am different
from who i was
way
back
when

i don't know
what comes next
but for now
there is peace
and for now
for now
i don't need to know
what comes next

AS YOU GO

let me
let go
of what's keeping
me from You
let me
let You
take what's keeping me
from You.

even when You answer
in a way different from my way
i'll continue to stay and say
You are the Way.

AS YOU GO

through the crack comes the light
and for a second i believe
everything will be alright
i'll be alright

lean into the
words He spoke
leave behind the
chains He broke
step forward with the
love He awoke

AS YOU GO

you are stronger than you think
you are stronger than you feel
you are stronger than before
you are stronger than you know

will You sit with me
as i sit with You
will You listen to me
as i speak to You
will You go with me
even when i try to go without
You

AS YOU GO

so this is what
it feels like to be free
to have my eyes wide
and heart open
with forward feet
seeking more than
all that was before

there's something about
words spoken with sincerity
that shake my soul awake
words placing promises
of forever and always
an honest reminder
that we are more
than our finest mistake
that we are more
than our finest mistake
that we are more
than our finest mistake

AS YOU GO

what if we just need to hear
we aren't a mistake
and there is more than all this
and it can be hard to breathe
but it's okay to breathe
and ask why
it's okay to breathe
and ask why
but it's okay to breathe
and ask why
it's okay to breathe

and i'll bring forward
all of me and
that's when i'll see
that You accept me
that You welcome me
that You sustain me
that You see me
that You know me
and known is all
i really want to be.

AS YOU GO

when it is the way
it was never supposed to be
take a moment to breathe
and remember the hope inside
that led you to be

hold on and don't let go
to this grace
that is bringing us home

AS YOU GO

there is
peace
in letting
go

i'll lean in
with a love
that cannot end
as i begin
to continue again

AS YOU GO

before me and beside
inside and out
it's You who is there
even when i doubt

let mercy
meet the
madness

AS YOU GO

and when the morning comes
i'll remember all You've done

when i stop
i see
it's You making
everything better
than it used to be

AS YOU GO

courage
be near
because
another day
is here

shape me with Your words
mold me with Your mercy
guide me back home
with Your grace alone

AS YOU GO

speak peace
straight into my soul
lean in loud
because
i want to feel the sound

TANNER OLSON

there
there is
there is joy
there is joy here.

AS YOU GO

young and afraid
waiting for the day
when i'm ready and brave
and maybe
just maybe
today is the day

i'm trying to be less like i was
and more like who i want to be.

i'm trying to hold onto the good
and do away with the bad.

and i'm trying to find my way
from the past to the present.

and i hope you know i'm just trying
to be better version of me
for you.

AS YOU GO

there is beauty
in the ordinary
but if i'm not looking
i'll never see
how You are part
of every little thing

i'm finding peace
in the morning light
waking early
to watch the sun rise
to see hope come alive
with my very eyes
slowing myself
before i pick up pace
to sit
and remember
God's glorious grace

AS YOU GO

when i am afraid
i'll give You my trust
with trembling hands
knowing You understand
and welcome me home
as i am.

it can be both heavy and light
and it can feel like the end
while beginning to believe
everything is going to be alright

AS YOU GO

let the silence fill this space
let patience keep me in this place
let my hands grip tight Your grace
whatever be the case
go with me as i run this race.

TANNER OLSON

i might be going
with my questions
but i'm not going alone
i'm going with the faith
that is bringing me home

AS YOU GO

as you go
may it be faith
that leads you
through the
unknown

as you go
may it be hope
that keeps you
moving through every
yes and every no

as you go
may it be love
you leave behind
so others may know
so others may grow
so others may go

AS YOU GO

As you go, remember to breathe.

Breathe.

Breathe in slowly.
Exhale slowly.

Again and again.

And again.

Breathing in the beauty that was seen and found.
Exhaling a day of ups and downs.
Or maybe it's a week or month of them.

Breathing in a faith that can move mountains.
Exhaling a mind that has moved miles.

Breathing in hope.
Exhaling heaviness.

Breathing in grace.
Exhaling peace.

Breathing in trust.
Exhaling control.

Know that He has it all under control.

Every little thing.

Breathe in slowly.
Exhale slowly.

And go.

As you go, go with hope.

ABOUT THE AUTHOR

Tanner Olson is an author, poet, and speaker living in Nashville, TN with his wife Sarah and their dog, Pancake.

Tanner started writing in 2013 and created the project Written to Speak. The mission of Written to Speak is to spread hope and announce love through written and spoken word poetry.

To bring Tanner to your next event, visit writtentospeak.com.

Instagram: @writtentospeak
Twitter: @tannerJolson
Support: patreon.com/writtentospeak

AS YOU GO

Thank you to my friends and family in Orlando, Wisconsin, St. Louis, Nashville, and Austin.

Thank you to those who have walked with me as this book was being written. You are written into every poem I've ever penned.

Thank you to James Saleska for designing this book and for your encouragement along the way.

Thank you to Kris Stack. I wouldn't be a poet if it wasn't for you.

Thank you to Justin Fricke and Adam Fricke for answering all my texts and calming my fears.

Thank you to Trevor Kunze. Let's go back to Germany.

Thank you to Jane and Aaron Littmann (and Boiler) for your constant love and prayers. Let's celebrate something soon.

Thank you to Rachel Wheatley, Taylor Jarman, Shelly Schwalm, Kelly Eaton, Rebekah Schumacher, Leah Abel, Lauren Moore, Brad Malone, Man Village, Camp Luther Family, LCMS National Youth Gathering Family, Nashville Family, the Williams Family, the Cohen Family, the Evans Family, the Willkom Family, the Eggebrecht Family, the Kasper Family, the Lane Family, the Bender Family, the Hickey Family, the Jackson Family, the Doering Families, the Klopke Family, the Grebing Family, and the Frazier Family for your friendship and constant encouragement.

Thank you to my family and friends who have become family. Your love and kindness continues to amaze me.

Thank you to our ACTS Church Network in Austin, Texas. You will always be our family.

Thank you to the Orlando Magic.

Thank you to Pancake for being the perfect dog. You are your own poem.

Thank you to my mom and dad and Tyler and Greta (and Caleb!). Without each of you I wouldn't be here. And neither would this book. I love you.

Thank you to Sarah Olson for editing the words I write. Like everything in my life, you make it better. Let's get married again. And go get donuts.

Thank you for reading this book.
I am honored that you would spend your time with these words.

If you'd like for me to come share poetry and stories at your school, church, conference, or organization, I would love to be there.

AS YOU GO

Thank you Patrons for helping bring this book to life.

- Aaron & Jane Littmann
- Abbie Snow
- Abigail López
- Alicia Houser
- Allison Serff
- Amanda
- Amanda Segebart
- Andrew Komurka
- Andrew, Marcia, Emma, & Celia Milam
- Eckert Family
- Angie Mortlock
- Anna
- April Kolman
- Ariel Capps
- Barbora Beňová
- Becca & Layne Johnson
- Bryan Fries & Family
- Bryan Moore
- Dave & Carol Helms
- Casen Lucas
- Caylan DeLucia
- Cedarburg Associates
- Cindy Arnold
- Connor Galloway
- Crystal Brutlag
- Dana Stigdon
- Dion Ordway
- Duane Highley
- Emily Garner
- Emily Henry
- Enean Mattes
- Elsie Servis
- Essie McCurdy
- Georgia Cameron
- Grace Benton
- Grace Hughey
- Grebing Family
- Greta Gieseke
- Hannah Nelson
- Hannah Ness
- Harry, Hannah, & Lionel Smith
- Heather Lancaster
- Heather Rose Gonzalez
- Heidi Galdes
- Jaimie Aliece
- Jan & Bruce Williams
- janelle
- Jennifer Castens
- Jill Bodling
- Jolene Berke

Jon Oestermeyer
Joy Hayward
Joy McLaughlin
Kaitlyn Saugstad
Katelyn McKeen
Kathleen Powell Moreno
Kelly McFarlin
Kim Pierson
Kurt Bimler
Laura Grimes
Lauren Moore
Linda Brink
Linda Sanborn
Lisa Grissinger
Dean & Lisa Olson
Luke Fitzhenry
Lynn Stack & Family
Macy Minniear
Matt & Jill Hewitt
Nea Kosonen
Nick Anderson
Nicolette McLaughlin
Phil & Erin Jones
Klopke Family

Preston & Savannah Roesslet
Rick & Brenda Masselink
Rhoden Family
Rosann Batteiger
Ruthie Buck
Sarah Bartok
Shelby Robinson
Susie P.
Suzie Katusky
Tanner Gerig
Tarah Agathe
Taylor Choate
Taylor & Mindy Jarman
Ted & Chelsey Doering
Tina Hoversten
Todd Nesloney
Tori Thibodeaux
Trevor & Kaitlin Kunze
Vicke Thrower
William & Alicia Jackson

As a Patron, you'll receive exclusive content and help support the mission of Written to Speak.

To become a Patron, visit patreon.com/writtentospeak

www.ingramcontent.com/pod-product-compliance
Lightning Source LLC
Chambersburg PA
CBHW051403290426
44108CB00015B/2141